IN A WHEELCHAIR

Chaplain Stephen C. Petrovich

WESTBOW
PRESS®
A DIVISION OF THOMAS NELSON
& ZONDERVAN

WestBow Press books may be ordered through booksellers or by contacting:

WestBow Press
A Division of Thomas Nelson & Zondervan
1663 Liberty Drive
Bloomington, IN 47403
www.westbowpress.com
844-714-3454

Interior Image Credit: Judy Grupp

Photography by Jose Seda

ISBN: 978-1-6642-6538-7 (sc)
ISBN: 978-1-6642-6539-4 (e)

Library of Congress Control Number: 2022908076

Print information available on the last page.

WestBow Press rev. date: 07/28/2022

Contents

Acknowledgements 1

Introduction... 3

A Mountain Flower 5

Jesus in a Wheelchair.. 6

Red River Valley Remembrance............................. 8

This Side of Heaven 11

The Language of Hands 13

Stripped Bare 14

Riddles of the Heart... 16

Don't Forget Our Love 18

Drawn to Her Personhood..................................... 20

Too Far Gone 23

Environmental Services... 25

Four Letters to Freedom.. 27

From One Soul to Another..................................... 29

I Kissed Heaven 31

A Nurse's Blessing... 32

A Lightning Bolt Experience 34

Love You Just the Same 37

Seeing Eye to Eye.. 39

Mother-Daughter Love 41

Once.. 43

A Seed, a Tree, an Axe, and Heaven....................... 45

Sacred Love... 47
The Best of Who You Are........................ 49
A Love Like Theirs 51
The Bumps in the Road........................... 53
The Joy of Solitude 55
A Thousand Goodbyes 56
A Social Worker's Tribute........................ 58
You're Transforming Me.......................... 60
Amazing... 63

Acknowledgements

Many thanks are necessary to the special people in my life. But 1ˢᵗ and foremost, I want to thank Jesus Christ for the gift of salvation, the inspiration of literature, and the guidance into the chaplaincy.

To my wife: I love you, Evelyn (MRS. P); you are my heart. God gave me the best when you became my wife.

To Chaplain Carolyn Nuthman, thank you for encouraging me to put my writings in a book.

To Fr. Robert Dagleish for planting a seed into my heart to develop my "BEAUTIFUL MIND."

To Fr. Eric Ockrin for being a friend, pastor, communicator, and reading many of my writings before anyone else.

To Mary Ann Esser, thank you for lending your intelligence, poetic sensibilities, educated opinions, and friendship to my writing. I appreciate your gifts. (Counselor and Teacher)

Also, to Jim and Mary Ann for love and support.

To Jesse Cruz, some agreed to edit my book to finish one. But, instead, you taught me how to edit one to write many.

To my Dad, "Eugene J. Petrovich," though you're

gone, I thank you for your love, the gift of discipline (Hebrews 12:11), and your interest in poetry that inspired me to write.

I love you, Mom. It's good to see you every day.

To my children (Jessica, Jason, Marie, Beth, and their spouses. Gerald, Angie, and Jon) and my grandchildren (Alyssa, Anaya, Aslan, Amari, Azariah, Airenaya, Aaliyah, Hayden, Alex, Hayley, and Jordan) you inspire me with your love, kisses and crazy antics. Prayers for all of you and my love forever.

And last but certainly not least, to the men and women I minister to daily. Your experiences, and love are treasures too good to be hidden, and so I honor you by sharing your stories with the world.

Introduction

Hello, I'm Chaplain Steve, and I invite you to walk with me through the hallways and into the rooms of dear hearts who need quality of life care. What I hope you'll find is compassion for your fellowman. Undoubtedly, you'll glimpse the "love" this world desperately needs.

Amongst the elderly population, I've found a treasure. Their stories alone are worth the time to visit. But the combination of love and loss resuscitates my heart in a world consumed with itself. Their lives need to be shared with everyone.

Another blessing I've discovered is the generosity from the caregivers. Their care is exceptional. The healthcare providers are giving "mini-bursts of love" every day to our residents. Self-sacrifice, honor and integrity are part of their daily routine.

So, come with me through the pages of Jesus in a Wheelchair and discover purpose and compassion from a new perspective. Where self-sacrifice and honor serve the least, the lost and the lonely.

One visit may not only change their world but yours as well.

A Mountain Flower

I told her, "You're a mountain flower."

She replied in a southern drawl, "I am?"

I said, "Yes, you have a sweetness about you."

She replied in a lilting voice, "I do?"

I said, "Yes." Then I knelt beside her bed so we could see eye to eye. She looked suspiciously at me, tilting her head ever so gently. I gazed back and explained, "A mountain flower blooms whether someone notices or not. It has a fragrance seldom appreciated. Yet, the breeze carries its scent through the hills-joining with various aromas of flowers and trees. It creates a bouquet that delights the senses. Can't you smell it?"

Then it dawned on her, and she whispered, "I'm a mountain flower?"

I nodded yes. To my delight, this southern belle's dimples danced across her face like the golden arch of the sun. Her heart soared, though, simultaneously, she struggled to straighten pieces of tissue to cover her incapacitated arm. She was my mountain flower.

Jesus in a Wheelchair

From across the hall, I heard a cry for help. As I entered the room, I saw a woman in a wheelchair whose face squeezed together like a sponge that soaked up a lifetime of tears. I was there to listen and possibly assist, but the woman's pain was beyond what I could comprehend. What did I do? I told her to let it out-let out the pain, release the frustration, unshackle the love. Then before my eyes, she released the weight of a thousand yesteryears. A saturation of life glistened on her face. Her eyes, nose, and mouth dripped.

Then her mouth slowly formed words that were like Morse Code to decipher: "I-love-the-Lord." Every word over accentuated her passion. Finally, I witnessed love in its purest form. Love that endures and reclaims its meaning in a world where the phrase "I love you" is thrown around haphazardly and without conscience. The moment languished, transcending time; her groans still fill my ears: "I love the Lord." The pain was the instrument through which she played her hymn of praise. This dear woman's pain bridged my pain; it became our device of communication and, in turn, our connection to our Savior's pain for us. Never had a Sunday morning sermon affected me with such intensity, so, through my tears, I joined in with her words: "I love the Lord." My life will never be the same, provided I remember this precious woman and how she assisted me to recognize Jesus in a wheelchair.

Red River Valley Remembrance

He asked me, "Do you know Red River Valley?"
I replied, "Actually, no."

Surprised, he exclaimed, "You don't?" So, he started singing with an aged voice in his wheelchair in the hallway. Yes, I heard his voice, but what I recognized was the sentiment behind the words. He sang of true love while others said, "she's going away." He knew Alzheimer's had stolen her memories, but by God Almighty, he was not going to forget her or their love. He was determined to remember for them both.

Reflecting upon her bright eyes, sweet smile, and how the sunlight glistened on her hair, he remembered all the years they shared. And he even remembered their garden. As he touched a photograph of younger days when they sat side by side on the green grass of summer, he slightly moved his head and said, "Hmm." Oh, he could remember. But now, all he had was a window into her soul through her eyes. And sometimes, an inkling of an understanding is resurrected when she hears "Red River Valley." The melody unlocks a memory in her heart, where she remembers once more and gazes back into her cowboy's eyes. I saw them in his room. I still hear the melody in the hallway. His love was unwavering, and his voice echoes in my ears of a cowboy who loved her so true.

This Side of Heaven

We gathered around her bedside, retelling stories and remembering the good ole days. Then, unbeknownst to us, this frail little saint became our teacher. She was showing us the way to die with dignity. First, she called upon Jesus and showered Him with love. Then she peacefully closed her eyes, and silence ensued. The honor to have lived near this woman of God was inspirational. Finally, I started to recite, "The Lord is my Shepherd," and to my disbelief, she opened her eyes and finished Psalm 23 word for word by herself.

I said, "You're becoming our teacher."

In response, she asked in a squeaky voice, "How much will you pay me?"

I was speechless; then, I chuckled. The three of us in the room—this little saints' son, the physical therapist, and I—just looked at each other in awe. Later I thought, I will remember to tell your story of faith to everyone I meet. And though it was impossible to pay for this experience, the treasure I believe she's received, is far more than any bank could hold this side of heaven.

The Language of Hands

After I sang "Amazing Grace" near her bedside, she asked, "May I hold your hand?" "Sure," I replied. I reached out my hand, and the elderly lady held it. The softness of her hand was like the petal of a tulip. It was delicate and warm. She repeatedly rubbed her thumb back and forth on the top of my hand. At first, I felt her loneliness; then, I sensed her tenderness. Her hand was an extension of her heart. When I took notice of her wrinkles, I could see her veins through the thinness of her skin. I could feel her pulse.

The emotional connection and the cure for loneliness were all contained in touch. As her oxygen tank rattled, she smiled and closed her eyes. After a few minutes, she released my hand and turned toward the window. The sunlight glimmered on her face.

"Thank you" is all she said.

I smiled and cordially dismissed myself.

Then she asked in a lilting quiver as I approached the door, "Come see me tomorrow?"

"Oh yes, as long as you hold my hand."

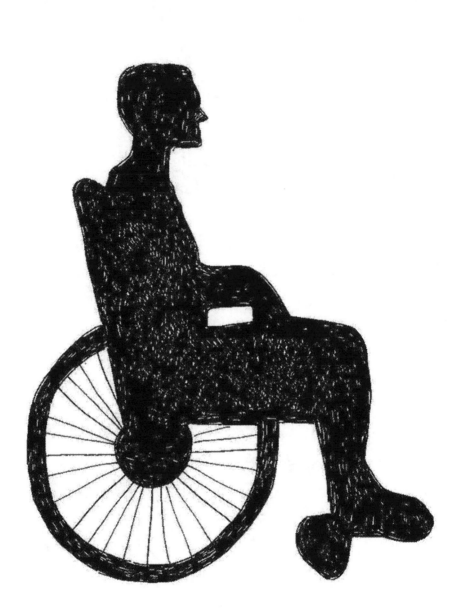

Stripped Bare

"How does it feel?" he asked.
"All I've ever acquired has been reduced to a bed, chair, T.V, dresser, and a

meagerly stocked closet in one room. How would you feel?" he retorted. "I had a home. I had a bank account. I had family, friends, faith, and freedom. Now all I have is faith, but I'm not sure if faith has me. Am I making sense? Sometimes, I believe; other times, I'm not sure. Often, I feel stripped bare. And it's only then the crucifixion of Christ becomes painfully clear. Of all His worldly attachments, Jesus was stripped, including His clothes. Job 1:21 states, 'Naked I came from my mother's womb, and naked shall I return there.'"

"I'm sorry, Chaplain. I'm comparing myself to people in the Bible and becoming a preacher to the preacher. But I do have a sense of connection to their plight. Sometimes I wonder if we're avoiding the obvious, so I won't beat around the bush anymore. Death is inevitable. I miss my spouse. The love we had was extraordinary. Now all I have are memories, and frankly, the missing hurts too much. The people here at the nursing home are friendly. But I feel in a strange way like an orphan invited to a family Christmas party. I receive gifts, but they don't feel like mine. I could go on rambling, and I'm sure you have plenty of people to visit so you can leave. But, as for me, I need to reconcile this reality myself. Thanks for listening."

As I go, I shudder to think of the pain and the heartbreak of being stripped bare.

Riddles of the Heart

 ere in this valley
There is such beauty
Rolling hills touch the sky

The trees reach with longing
Each branch like fingers
Pointing my heart to ask why

Who makes the sunshine?
And who sends the rain?
Who makes the flowers bloom in the spring?
Who writes the riddles on the heart of man?
And when the darkness finds me will I see the light
again?

White-tailed deer disappear
As the forest closes around them
Hooting owls drown out the sound
Of the loneliness deep inside of me

Who makes the wind blow?
And who sends the snow?
Who walks beside me when senses grow old?
And who writes the riddles on the heart of man?

And when the light shines upon me
If...the light shines upon me
Will I find life in your eyes?

Don't Forget Our Love

I was visiting a couple at a senior living home. They still held hands; it touched my heart. You knew love was in the room. Their smiles were still aglow though wrinkles lined their face. And somehow, I intruded in a very public place. "After fifty years of marriage," I asked, "how could this be?"

Then, leaning over, he winked at her and said these words to me.

"She said, 'Don't forget our love.' That's what she said to me. 'Don't forget our love; it's in my heart eternally.' She said, 'Though I won't remember, please remember what I've said. Don't forget our love.'"

As I wiped my eyes, I tried to act so brave, but he took his fist like a manly man and lightly tapped my face.

He said, "Slugger, she's easy to love, and many years ago, when she found me lost and broken, she kind of saved my soul. "If not for her, I would never be the man I am today. So, if you wonder why I do what I do, it's what she used to say.

She said, 'Don't forget our love.' That's what she said to me. 'Don't forget our love; it's in my heart eternally. Though I won't remember, please remember what I've said. Don't forget our love.'"

He said, "As the years go by, this ole heart still feels the sting. But this love could never be replaced by anyone or anything.

'Don't forget our love.' That's what she said to me. 'Don't forget our love; it's in my heart eternally.' Though she can't remember, I remember what she said. Don't forget our love."

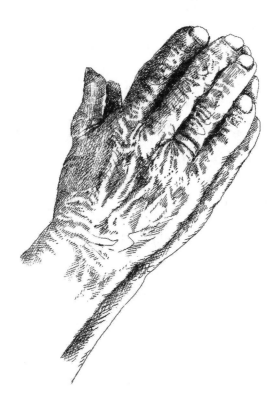

Drawn to Her Personhood

I observed a woman whose body was twitching in a wheelchair while I sang "You Are My Sunshine." After I finished singing, I approached. The disease twisted her body in such a way that I assumed her voice represented the same, but before I could introduce myself, she read my name tag and said, "Stephen."

Surprised, I said, "Hello," then asked, "What's your name?" When she articulated her name, tranquility filled the hallway, and I was drawn to her personhood more than her disabilities.

"I'm the chaplain, uh … may I pray for you?" Then her face contorted with a twist of the neck as if to align herself as she continued to speak.

"Pray, pray for me," she pleaded. Whatever sights or sounds were in the hallway couldn't intrude on this holy moment. It was her, me, and God meeting on hallowed ground for mercy, grace, and healing.

I started, "In the name of the Father," her body was making the sign of the cross. "In the name of the Son-with each word, her head, arms and legs moved side to side. "In the name of the Holy Spirit," I touched her shoulder, and she shot up rigid. It shocked me. Her belief stirred my faith. There was an expectation, and I thought to myself I'd better be present. Then she repeated herself. "Pray, pray." There was an acceleration. Her desperation sucked the air from the hallway. As humbly as I could, I proclaimed the name that's above every name, "Jesus." As I looked upon this dear woman, my savior came to mind. He was chastised, mangled, and obliterated willingly for my sake. And He laid dead, in the arms of His mother. This woman's body was as good as dead, but her soul was at peace after prayer. As a result, she awakened in me a deeper understanding of hope and reconciliation through presence and intercession.

Too Far Gone

He looked me straight in the eye and said, "I don't care what you say, what you believe, or how you're looking at me. I'll do what I do because I did what I did. There's no turning back; I won't keep my feelings in. Though it feels like I'm dying, I'll live with it, and I'll deal with it, oh forget it. I'm a runaway train. I've got no one to blame but myself. There's a hundred thousand miles of sin and mistakes behind me. My punishment are these rattlesnakes in my body. Their poison is burning me up. My body convulses, I'm reeling in pain, the torture is relentless, and there in my brain are a million regrets from my choices of yesterday. This is my payment for my pleasure. This is my suffering for my sin. I don't trust myself, and I won't let anyone in. So, you can save all your secondhand philosophies. I've made my bed, that's where you'll find me. I'm too far gone.

I knew the consequences. My choices got me right where I am. Too many parties, too much fun-I knew what I was doing; I knew it was wrong. So, don't feel sorry for me. Nobody cares anyway. And if someone did, I don't think I would. I appreciate your gesture. I guess I'm thankful for the prayer, or at least for the intention. But I'm too far gone."

Environmental Services

You may feel like you're invisible as you clean rooms and disinfect toilets. But as you take out the trash, soiled clothes, then change your gloves, you're changing more than you may know. Your service is adding value to our residents' lives. The atmosphere is better. It certainly smells fresh and clean because of you. Besides the healthy environment, your demeanor can change someone's day, and all I want to say is thank you. Your smile is worth its weight in gold.

Environmental services is affecting me, and it's logical to think others take notice too. You're assisting in the care of each resident you are encountering. This facility can't function without you because the residents can't heal or thrive in an unhealthy environment. So, your work is as necessary as any other professional on the campus. Please accept my deepest gratitude for the work you do. You are genuinely essential to the health of this facility, and because you give your best, others can rest and have a clean-living environment.

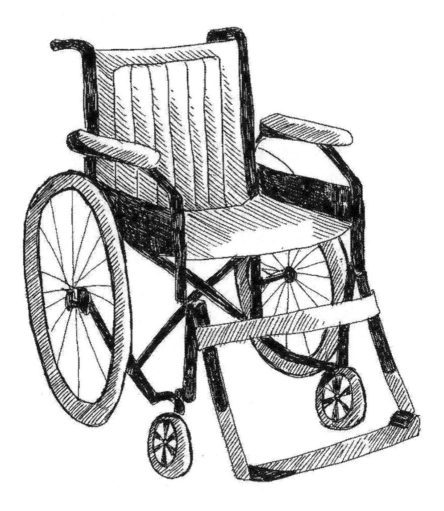

Four Letters to Freedom

I saw four letters on the chalkboard.

P.T.O.T.

Little did I know these letters spell hope. As the physical therapist, you administer hope through physical therapy and occupational therapy. When I see your smile and hear how you greet each care recipient, I perceive an individual who didn't show up just for a paycheck. Your desire to assist with their limited mobility is your highest priority, and the residents are encouraged by your sincerity. But there's more than meets the eye in all you do. You have a terrific combination of practical application coupled with an empathetic heart. You not only bring hope, but you embody optimism. Your cadence is one of belief with the possibility of new physical strength, maneuverability, and confidence.

You teach the patient how to do things that once were easy. And I see how the hard work pays off. People are walking again. People are pivoting and getting into vehicles with little or no assistance. Your knowledge, skill, and exercises are blessing individuals that may groan about the challenges, but in the end, your reward is their independence. P.T.O.T. are four letters to freedom.

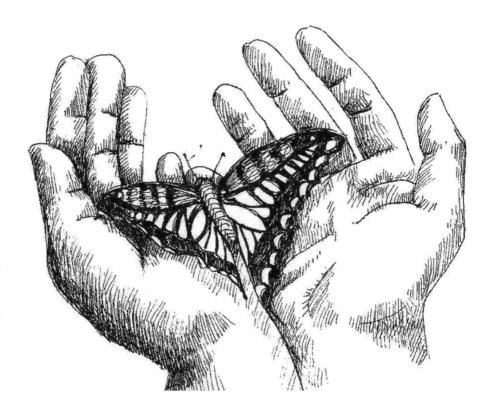

From One Soul to Another

You know, if I could, I would care for my own body, but I am unable. And I hope you know I would thank you, but sometimes I can't even do that. It's humbling and kind of humiliating because I feel worthless, but you give me worth. I feel powerless, but you empower me. When I'm confused, you bring clarity. When I'm disappointed, you offer hope. Sometimes I feel like giving up, but you inspire me to live. You make me feel better about myself. I have value in your eyes, and in your hands, I feel safe.

You lift me when I'm down, and because of your care, I have life. Your effort and sacrifice have not gone unrecognized; you're an outstanding care provider. I need you. If you're ever discouraged, call to mind all you've done for me. Then, reread these words, and in your remembering, please accept my love—from one soul to another.

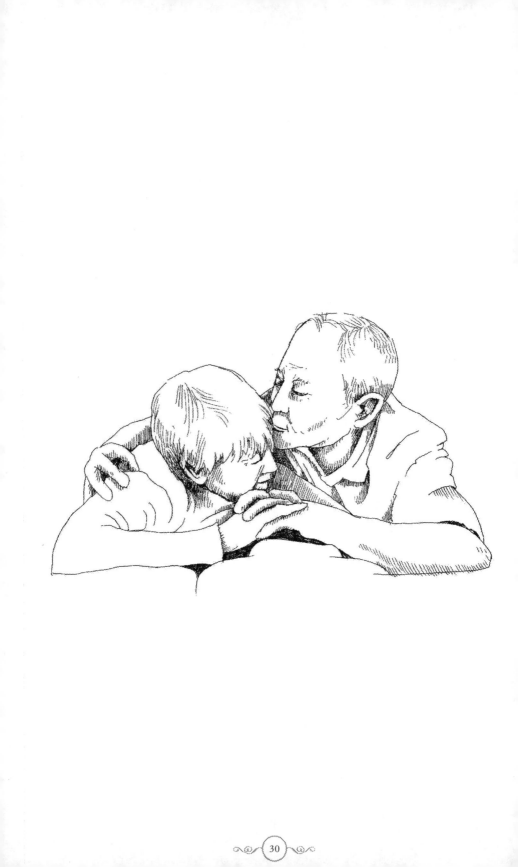

I Kissed Heaven

She was weak, and Heaven was calling. I asked, "How are you?" Through the oxygen mask, she tried to speak but smiled instead. Recognizing her difficulty, I asked, "May I hold your hand?" Her eyes lit up, and she opened her hand. I sat beside her, and we relished the silence. Time stood still. She looked at me, and I looked at her; then, to my surprise, she placed her other hand on top of mine. So, I was inclined to ask, "May I kiss your forehead?" Humbly she nodded. Gently, I let go of her hand, stood up, brushed her white hair from her wrinkled forehead, and kissed it.

I couldn't miss the opportunity to show appreciation for our precious little chats. Then, sensing the finality of the moment, I wondered aloud, "What are you thinking about?" This time despite the oxygen mask and with all the strength she could muster, she responded, "I'd like to do it all over again." I just smiled because, honestly, I couldn't comprehend what "do it all over again" would encompass. The next day I visited, she was gone, but I'll never forget the day I kissed Heaven.

A Nurse's Blessing

our work touches lives; your efforts matter. Amid the stress and tug of responsibility you feel, a dormant call button serves as a lifeline for a care recipient counting on you. It lies on the bed like a security blanket or a guardian providing the patient with access to your heart. The peace they feel knowing you'll be available is indescribable to the patients. And there are far too many needs. You have your own needs, but you answered a calling deep within. What made you care in the first place? Was it a memory of a loved one? Or is it something that gives life when you give to those in need? The inspiration may be a mystery, but your work, passion, and caring are blessing the least of these. According to Aristotle, the hand is the tool of tools. Your hands are blessed; each finger works together for the consolation of a soul.

You stretched out your hand toward the trembling hand of the needy. And with your hands, you show generosity, strength, and stability. You're appreciated. You're cherished; you really are. I hope every "thank you" and smile you receive from residents fill your heart with satisfaction and joy. And even when you don't receive thanks, your presence alone was like a star, lighting up someone's darkest night who needed you most. The heart of a nurse is like no other. It's a creation all its own. It beats with compassion, is unmatched in service, and is filled with blessings.

A Lightning Bolt Experience

I came into his room and introduced myself. We made small talk for a while until he asked about the guitar on my back. He once played banjo and loved folk music, so I cut into "This Land is Your Land." His fingers twitched as if he was playing along, and I believe he went back to a happier time before his sickness. I asked about his faith, and he said he was Jewish, but he never practiced or prayed.

Instead, he said, "I was waiting for my lightning bolt experience."

I told him my testimony in so many words, paused-then with a still small voice; I said, "God loves you." It caught him off guard; now, his face responded as his fingers did earlier when I played guitar.

He said, "I hope God loves me." I started to move closer towards his bedside. I placed my hand on his shoulder and replied, "Oh, He does love you, and I see it's affecting you by the way your eyes are getting misty." Just then, a single tear streamed down his cheek. It was like I was in a maternity ward. The room was electric.

Then I asked, "May I pray?" he replied in a quivery voice, "Sure." I told him the God of Abraham, Isaac, Jacob, and the Messiah were drawing him closer. At this, his face lit up, and with tears rolling down his cheeks, he sheepishly smiled. So, I reached out and shook his hand, looked him in the eyes, and said, "I believe this was your lightning bolt experience!"

Love You Just the Same

Sometimes when I'm on the road listening to the radio, I remember you. And tears fill up the side of my eyes, and like a cup in the hand of an afternoon drunk, they spill. I remember the good times and sometimes the not so good, but I always recollect that your love was real. I know, without a shadow of a doubt, that you were proud of me. And I'm thankful for a dad who held me in his arms and showed me how to love. That was a gift!

From this perspective, I do what I do as a chaplain. I'm assisting people in the most challenging times with the compassion I learned as a child. But memories can be complicated, causing much pain for the joy of reminiscing beautiful things, like playing guitar and bicycling, is coupled with strict lessons and harsh discipline. Nevertheless, I am who I am because God chose you to be my dad. And whether for good or bad, I love you just the same.

Seeing Eye to Eye

Please excuse me, but I'm not just some cranky old person. Once upon a time, I had a life of my own, I worked hard, I had a home. You should ask me about my adventures; I'll share those I can remember. Oh, the people I met and the places I've seen. I was loved; I hope I still am. I had purpose and meaning in my life. But now, my body has deceived me; it's my own worst enemy.

I can't do what I used to do. I can barely walk, and I need help getting dressed. Getting old is terrible; I can hardly feed myself. People expect more from me, and sometimes when I try, the pain is unbearable. So, today if I'm grouchy, walk a mile with my walker. Lay in a soiled diaper for a while, then come back and talk to me about cranky. Maybe we'll laugh. Or perhaps we'll cry, but I think we'll see eye to eye.

Mother-Daughter Love

She uses a walker from her car to the room of her daughter. She brings a gift; no billionaire could afford. But there's no gift wrap or bows. Oh, the world doesn't know how it sparkles much more than diamonds. And what they have will last beyond the hands of time.

It's a mother's heart; it's an endless love; it can reach the unreachable star. It brings hope against all odds; it's a mother-daughter love. In all of creation, it's one of God's most beautiful gifts. It's a mother-daughter love.

Her fingers once danced so delicately across the ivories. Where the melodies of Mozart and Chopin filled the air. But now, this fair maiden is ill, but it can't break the will of her mother. So, she'll love higher and longer, deeper and stronger. She'll sacrifice all for the love of her daughter, for not even death could ever stop this love.

It's a mother's heart; it's an endless love; it can reach the unreachable star. It brings hope against all odds; it's a mother-daughter love. In all of creation, it's one of God's most beautiful gifts. It's a mother-daughter love.

Once

Once she needed eyes of faith, but now in Heaven, she sees. Once, she needed CNAs to attend to her every need. Once, she had loved ones who faced fears and shed tears long before she left. But now she knows the fullness of glory, for now in glory she's kept. Once upon a time sounds so cliché, but if we could bend our ear. What do you think she'd say to you? What would she want us to hear?

She might say, "My journey's over." She might say, "I miss you all." But I'm sure she would say, "Once I was in need, and you answered a noble call. Thank you, I will love you forever.

A Seed, a Tree, an Axe, and Heaven

The war to end all wars sowed a seed of sadness. The blood-soaked ground encapsulated the sound of the brother you loved. Your feelings were numb, and your spirit so young longed for stability, but instead, the church betrayed you. If an earthly father faltered, how could you ever believe in a Heavenly Father? Wrinkled and worn, body thin, the hourglass was seen by all. And the seed, a tree that supported your life, you fear it must fall. How can you live if the tree comes down? It's where you've staked your claim. The ax is heavy, the body weak, and heaven calls your name.

Another tree, its branches unseen, was transplanted near your soul. Though the root is small, it goes under the wall that surrounds your field of woe. A lesson learned; a message spurned soon a man will birth. Because of the revelation of his own need as heaven touches earth. Your brother's blood then sings from the ground. You hear it from a distant land. Forgiveness and grace, remarkable faith, brother, now take my hand.

Sacred Love

I see love-know love and experience love when I observe couples whose circumstances are uncomfortable-when it seems unbearable, and all that's left are memories. Tomorrow once represented the joy of knowing absolute unity. Now the future is endurance and uncertainty, where grieving is an active emotion mixed with a promise and a vow to love for better, for worse.

This portrayal of love is compelling. True love captivates; perfect love annihilates fear. It moves love from its eggshell fragility of infatuation to a love that stands firm even when death is imminent. This love empties itself for the sake of the beloved, a love that's stronger than death. It's reminiscent of cosmic love, which moved time and space, which made man eternal by a love that caused God to incarnate. I'm a witness to this mystery. This love is worthy of sacrifice; it's sacred love.

The Best of Who You Are

When faced with challenging conditions, you have shown self-control, professionalism, and a positive attitude. Your gifting as a nurse is admirable. Your training is evident, and your compassion is exceptional. "Thank You" may not seem adequate for all you do, but thank you, nonetheless.

Your diligence inspires, and your professionalism raises our standards of care. Your commitment to the needy is noteworthy, especially when residents become anxious or agitated. What you do matters, and how you do it matters to patients, coworkers, and anonymous passersby. We appreciate your decision to partner with us. You have an exemplary work ethic that reinforces our core values of healthcare. The best of who you are inspires the best of whom we can be.

A Love Like Theirs

Somewhere in there, he's still aware. His movement is slothful. His pain is evident, but the peace he exudes is prevalent. Because his words are few, his heart communicates love. And though his strength is gone, grace allows him to hold on. Oh, for the mercy he's shown. May mercies return a hundredfold.

The years haven't been kind but, in the midst, he's found the love of his life. She's, his advocate. And you'd be better off to cross a mother bear in the wild. Why? Because love lays down its life, but not without a fight. And their treasure to the world is a sanctified image of marriage. It reaches further than time and space. It stretches beyond, and it's not out of place to declare that every soul longs to know a love like theirs.

The Bumps in the Road

Don't do that to yourself. Second-guessing and questioning your ability will get you nowhere. It drains energy from your soul. Instead, recognize how far you've come; this is just the beginning of your journey to greatness. You've got heart. You have tenacity. Your untapped ability is surging with every struggle you're experiencing. Be encouraged. God made you with determination; that's why the darkness can't stop you. You're an overcomer. You've got grit; move on and take it in stride.

So, what if you hit a bump in the road? What if those hurdles are the missing ingredient to your destiny? Life's a breeze when all goes well, but it seems you engage a new gear when challenges arise. Then you capitalize and become more distinguished because of adversity. So, remember, even when you encounter obstacles on the way to the finish line, you'll make it because you're a champion. Never forget that! You're moving in the right direction, and your destination is more significant because of the bumps in the road.

The Joy of Solitude

I enter as if there were a door, and stillness greets me. I hang up my cares and proceed through a hallowed hallway. I sit in silence as thoughts of yesterday combined with the responsibility of today clamor for attention. I'm served a glass of solitude and empty my mind. I meditate using a mantra, "The joy of the Lord, the joy of the Lord."

Silence inspires peace, tranquility, and restoration follow. Intentionally, I breathe deep, and a calming satisfaction envelops me. Thankfulness rises; peace continues with confidence. Joy, joy, joy–the words like rocks in a shallow stream glisten in my mind. The sun shimmers, and reflections resonate in my spirit where I discover the joy of solitude in the presence of the Lord.

A Thousand Goodbyes

Every day I go to work, it's the same pattern. I knock at the door, introduce myself, get acquainted; then (with my head held low), I say another eulogy. I call it a thousand goodbyes. It sounds harsh, but it's a reality as a chaplain or any healthcare provider for that matter. That's why these poems and reflections are so important to me. They allow me to grieve and say goodbye at my own pace. It's strange, but sometimes I feel their presence when I visit someone who's in their old room. I remember our conversations and their stories. I recall the laughter, tears, and emotional struggles. And when God collected their tears in bottles, I dried their face.

I'm honored to work hand in hand with God, but the flip side of every blessing is a curse. That's too strong a word, but that's just the way it feels. Let me explain. I see people at their most vulnerable. They're in pain, and I feel that pain. It hurts, and I feel powerless.

Then, I experience how God shows up and comforts them. The juxtaposition causes an emotional seesaw of blessings and curses. Amid describing my ministry as a thousand goodbyes, I feel like I'm becoming more calloused to death. I think I do this for self-preservation and sanity. Only time will tell. Healthcare work (life, death, and grieving) for the elderly is serious business. And by God's grace, I intend to be present to each resident amongst a thousand goodbyes.

A Social Worker's Tribute

Who is this person who seems to spin multiple responsibilities simultaneously, giving equal attention and consideration to all? A Social Worker is a miracle worker with countless blessings at their fingertips to disperse. At the speed of light, fingers document the needs, the progress, and the prognosis for the best care plan of the patient. Loving inhabits your day where strangers become friends, and because of your gifting, friends become family. You give of your time, skipping meals and rearranging schedules for the benefit of others. What a gift! Where would we be without social workers who give their hearts, souls, and strength away? The power of community is what you bring to the lonely, returning honor to the outcast and restoring healing to the downtrodden. Your care is worth far more than you're compensated, yet it was never about the money. It was always about your heart, including gifts of attentiveness and love. So, today, receive this recognition. Here's a pat on the back and a tip of the hat.

Your ability to arrange, organize and vision for a helpless soul is significant. Your compassion inspires and your sensitivity advances acts of kindness. Exactly what you need to accomplish your job, is precisely what you have. And that makes you a terrific social worker. We are far better off because of you!

You're Transforming Me

How do I stay true to my convictions while guiding others with unorthodox or non-existent belief systems? It's a burden, and even more, it's unnerving. I'm feeling tugged like a rope in a spiritual tug of war between secularism and Christianity. The turbulence is alarming. It's a war between God and the world, where man is the unsuspecting casualty. Of course, God wins; but it's not without pain, including the crucifixion and rejection of His love and forgiveness. So, what does all this do for me? Even more, what does it do to me? It certainly creates a barrage of unanswered questions. How can I treat others' beliefs the same as Christianity? And if I do, will I offend my savior? I don't know what to do! I'm experiencing mental anguish, which is the crux of the dilemma. I never want to minimize the God I love by crediting false belief-they considered trustworthy.

First off, don't try to figure this all out in a split second. Wrestle with it. What am I saying to you in the wrestling? Who are you becoming because of the struggle? Don't fear or doubt the process— stand firm. Be ever-loving and remember your origin. Did you always believe accurately or live out your faith appropriately? Find common ground and season your words with hope. Be mindful of My presence; I am with you. I wouldn't guide you into this position without provision. Enter the tension. You're okay. I'm a friend of sinners-I make a way in the wilderness when there's no way, and I'll give you all the necessary words to say as I transform you.

Amazing

I looked at myself in the mirror, passed the wrinkles beyond the grey, and told myself, "You are amazing; absolutely amazing!" Now some may think this is vanity. Some may consider it pride, but what we believe about ourselves has merit in our lives. Each of us is amazing! We're all unique. No one is like you; you have a specific set of circumstances that make up your identity.

Your mind is brilliant, your character a delight, and your smile is infectious and disarming, especially when you say hello to strangers. You're exceptional because of your humble demeanor in the presence of the Lord. You allow His Spirit to lead even when you don't understand. You're growing wiser as you get older. Despite time affecting your bones with all those aches and pains, you're getting better with age. You take challenges in stride. You're even allowing confrontational encounters to awaken an empathetic heart for others. You should celebrate! You've matured, you're not resting on your laurels, you're pressing in, and you believe in a glorious future. Now, look again into the mirror; You are AMAZING!

Printed in the United States
by Baker & Taylor Publisher Services